silence

Dedicated to my grandmother, who suffered in silence,
and to the friends, family, and supporters
who helped me break my own.

Thank you.

silence

POETRY, PHOTOS & A F**K TON OF FEELINGS

Camilla Nicole Petyn

Innards

Motel 6	1
Autopsy	2
Daffodils in a Pickle Jar	4
Vulnerability #1	6
Breathing Holes	8
Ms. Masochist	9
Hipbones Made of China	10
My Box	14
Claustrophobia	15
Come Hither	16
The Mad Creator	19
Existential Nonfiction	20
Small Talk	23
Virgin	25
Can I Have A Drag?	26
Pellucid Possessions	28
Cremation Creation	30
Deadly Lover	31
Interplay	35
Darkness, Personified	36
Ugly	37
Silence	38
The Word	40
Symphony	43
Grown From Dirt	44
Your Ravaged Painting	47

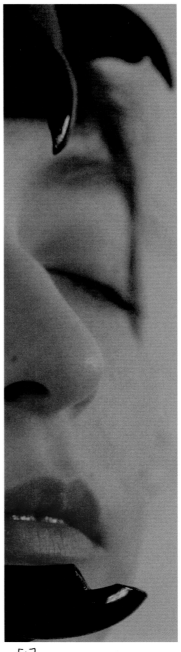

Scissors — 48

Leaky Faucet — 49

My Straight Jacket — 53

The Rotten Peach — 55

Vulnerability #2 — 57

Back Magic — 60

Swimming/Drowning — 61

It's Been A Year — 63

Bottle-Bound — 65

Cemetery Revelations — 66

World Shattering Hips — 68

Coffee Cake Lovers — 69

Little Pill — 71

The Intimate Chihuahua — 73

Deeper Into The Labyrinth — 77

Don't Forget To Be Yourself! — 79

Zits — 83

Dear Vicious Cycle — 84

Time To Thaw — 85

Malformed Fingers — 86

The Tell-Tale Half Smile — 88

A Bite of Blues — 91

Immortal — 93

Acknowledgments — 95

Index (photographers, models, etc.) — 97

Resources — 98

Dear reader,

I consider this book to be the inside of my mind. And let me tell you, it is a very personal (and terrifying) thing to share your innermost thoughts.

I originally wrote these pieces as a form of purge, to rid myself of any emotion or memory I couldn't manage metabolizing. I sat in Icelandic coffee shops, while rain and wind brawled, trying to understand my yearn via words. I wandered through Swiss forests, finding the perfect mound of earth, planted my darkened brain and grew rhymes. This book has gone to many places with me (or rather I've gone with this book), but wherever I was, I never drifted from the original desire of wanting to express and understand the things I felt. But, the reason I share them with you now is in hopes that you feel and connect with my words and therefore you can metabolize. I say these are "my words" but in reality, the moment you read them- they are yours. I also had a strong urge to pair many poems with photographs. Their purpose serves the same purpose of all art- to be enjoyed and felt.

I also feel the need to include a **trigger warning**. I pull a great amount of my inspiration from my own turmoil, physical and mental, so some of the topics included are: suicide, depression, addiction and eating disorders. If you find yourself sensitive to any of these topics, maybe reconsider reading and (if you haven't already) look into getting yourself the help you deserve. Nobody deserves to live in agony.

I've left some resources in the back.

Break your silence.

— C

I've always questioned
whether art is an expression of insanity
*or rather just the key **to** sanity.*

Motel 6

The ashtray shattered
while my mother slept fifteen miles away,
wrapped in cotton lies.
And I watched Michael silently
in room number 8,
surrounded by stolen liquor bottles
and the sound of cracking drywall.

I'd never seen veins
so maddened before.
As if with every pulse
they threatened to sprout
arms through Michael's skinny neck
and tear open my virgin skin
to search for the syringe he lost.

I remained silent.
I think that was the most silent
I've ever been.

Seven holes. His fist. Another vein.
Now, eight.

Autopsy

If you began at my skull
with a sharpened scalpel
and ran it down my throat,
through my sternum, and then
to the bottom of my stomach,
what would you find?

I'd lay filleted like a fish, carcass spread
open to remove the undesirable.
In place of a brain, you'd find rags
spoiled, a rotting yellow. I have tried
to wipe up too many messes here.

I might then ask you to sink your blade
deeper, maybe give it a twist
in the middle of my breast bone.
"Hallelujah!" I would scream.
Flailing my limbs in hopes
that I'd begin foaming at the mouth
while a beast roars out, ripping
my ribcage. I wish it were that easy.

And then I'd laugh once
you arrived at my stomach.
I know what you'd find here.

The cement that has possessed
the organ since October.

The acid hatred that pierced my tongue
every night I dug into my esophagus.
Maybe you'd even find some hope,
fermenting in vodka.
And if you dug deep enough you'd find
all the swallowed pleas and cries,
now just silent martyrs.

Daffodils in a Pickle Jar

I held my fork, ready for battle.
Between us sat two plates and nine daffodils
blooming in an empty pickle jar.

The swollen eye struggled to remain open and my leg
shook incessantly under the oaken table,
a desperate attempt to dissolve my anger.
It didn't work. I held my fork like a spear. And yelled.
"Why couldn't you have told me?"

She looked up from her untouched plate,
her face painted with the fraud confusion all moms master.
It didn't work. She gripped her spoon. And replied.
"It was for your own good."

I could feel my face singe,
I knew that would be the answer.
But I was disappointed and embarrassed and pissed off
and needed someone to blame.

"Why couldn't you have told me to not kiss
boys who love needles more than me,
or not to trust girls that dump water on moldy lies,
or maybe just how to throw a fucking punch?"

Then there was silence,
minus the noise behind our skulls.
"What if" scenarios blasting like a drive-in movie.

My mom spoke first.
"If I did, you would have
never become the daffodil who
blooms in a pickle jar."

Vulnerability #1

Sour in my mouth,
tongue shuns contact
out of fright.

Breathing Holes

You used to catch spiders in plastic cups,
watched their bodies decompose
without breathing holes. So, when you stabbed
the lid of mine, I began to believe
I was favored.

(I might thank you for the suffocation one day,
now knowing I refuse to live within
anybody's cup of insecurities,

with or without breathing holes.)

Ms. Masochist

Whose nails are these, digging
into the apple of my skin?
Arousing this latency.

How desperately they grip,
drawing blood and distraction.

"Oh yeah, you like that, baby?"

I dig deeper.

Hipbones Made of China

This reflection came with a mortgage.
My name no longer on the title,
I pay with my decay.

Sometimes handfuls of hair are my currency.
Occasionally a burnt throat or a nosebleed.
Or even my shins and kneecaps, coated
with purple, yellow, green war paint.
(Always hidden, by the way).
Maybe one day I'll pay with rotten teeth,
or my breath.

Expensive,
but at least I can see my hipbones.

here's a secret:

it's
not
worth
it.

It never will be.

Just love your body.

Please.

My Box

There isn't much room in here,
in this box of mine.

My head remains bowed,
my torso drawn in to fit. And the floor
reeks of mildew. A reincarnation.

Some days, better days,
I place my hand on the lid and push.
But then I let it slam shut.
I've found comfort in the discomfort.

Claustrophobia

It's the holidays that are always the most claustrophobic. The walls tend to sink inward while fireworks explode over crowds of linked arms and flag-patterned paper cups. And it's when I should be blowing out candles, ironically, the oxygen becomes thin. It's during the costume party or the Cinco De Mayo margaritas or even the damn Labor Day BBQ that people like us are sitting at home, silent, with the word "loner" wrapped around our throats.

Come Hither

Empty spaces beckon me.
"It's okay, come hither."
Their tongue soft,
it caresses me.

"We have no fingers to wag,
no eyes to roll,
we will never shun"
the emptiness says
with whispers like melted sugar.

The Mad Creator

There's a certain madness in the creative process: a lone hunched back lit only by a computer screen, like a church statue after hours. The sigh of defeat as reign is given up to the ricocheting thoughts of synonyms and syllables, trampling over any thought of sleep. Or the damp shirt sleeve(s), accompanied with snot and a mound of crumpled paper.

And yet, the creator still persists through it all. With the only reason being- the pursuit of creation. It's a bit mad. But as Alice one said: "the best people are." And I believe that goes for art, as well.

Existential Nonfiction

Occasionally, when in the company of
merlot and a mirror,
solitude-induced thoughts
lock me with my own gaze.

I don't know how long I sit
in this silly crouch, face inches
from the glass, begging my eyes
to give away answers.

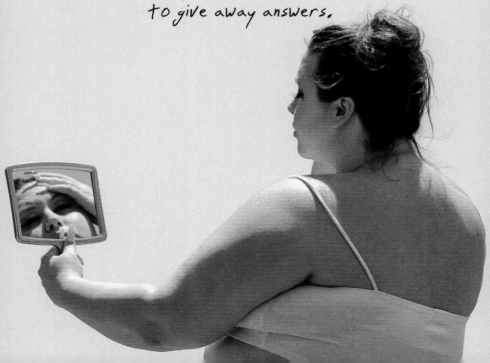

All I know is that

my pupils are damn stubborn.

Small Talk

There's something
excruciatingly vulgar
about violence,

yet if "small talk"
had a physical form
I would gladly
choke it out
with its own
hollow tongue.

Virgin

A young blonde virgin
lying in her bed
salivating for lack
of sobriety.

I suppose
titles can be
a bit misleading
sometimes.

Can I Have A Drag?

(thoughts from an ex-smoker)

Why? So you can be death's little whore?
So you can get on your knees and hold
The Reaper himself within your lips
until he comes and you feel
whole again, momentarily?

Or maybe it's because you're lonely.
Slender pale fingers meet
their slender pale companion.
How romantic.
How pathologically romantic.
Two broken don't make a whole,
unless one is willing to step forward.
And you can't step forward
while stuck in tar.
You can only fight your way out.

"Can I Have A Drag?"

How ironic that the flimsy cardboard box
presents its occupants' acts of villainy
yet doesn't mention the most vital.
WARNING:
CAUSES CANCER OF THE MOUTH.
WARNING:
THIS PRODUCT CONTAINS CHEMICALS
KNOWN TO CAUSE BIRTH DEFECTS.
Where's the warning for complete utter loss of sight?
WARNING:
YOU WILL THINK THIS IS YOUR FRIEND.

Friends don't make friends chew
their fingernails bloody
while waiting for an answer to
"Can I Have A Drag?"

(He said yes
and handed me his cigarette.
We both stood in silence,
closing our eyes,
covering our ears,
inhaling.)

Pellucid Possessions

Come, come!
Look, look!
Drool over my
shiny things
as I shower
in your spittle
with hopes to grow.

Cremation Creation

I wish ashes would fall
as you sit in the midst
of their black parade.

A beautiful sight it would be.
A downpour of the past
smoldering around you,
leaving no stains.

You'd sit with the used match.
I'd hold your hand.

I wish those ashes would fall.
I wish to one day see such a birth.

Deadly Lover

Occasionally, as morning fends off the night,
and I've stared at these blank walls too long,
Death comes to visit.

And he shoves his tongue down my throat and pulls
away slowly, whispering "don't worry, you always have me."
And I can't resist moaning.

Interplay

Round and round they go,
gambling away physicality
for a spot atop
news reporters' tongues
and within our delicate
skull sponges.

What a monotonous interplay.
They act, we react.
They stab, we succumb
to the media saturation
on silver screens,
while they paint big bloody X's

on movie theaters and concert halls
that we dare not now step foot.
But, we can't hide forever.
Plus, it reeks of agony in here
and the walls are stained
with grief.

Round and round they go,
gambling and pulling triggers.
Round and round we must go,
living, breathing and refusing
to remember their names.

Darkness, Personified

Enigma escaped the confines
of her defining pages.
She mortally roams
doused in her
once enveloping wording.
Dressed in black,
she sits with me.

"Where did you come from?"
I ask her.
"I came from you,"
she answers.
"I do not know you,"
I defend.

She smiles, used to being
tied and gagged,
created non-fictional by bit lips
and quivering fingertips.
She leans in closer,
cupping my cheek with a cold palm,
"One day you will know me.
And one day you will see you are a flame,
strong and clear beside me."

Ugly

I hate to be the one to break it to you,
but sometimes, growth is damn ugly.
There's nothing pretty about
smashing plates or beloved constructs.
Or being burned by the steam
coming from our lover's ears.
Nobody desires swollen eyes or
sticky hands or sweaty foreheads
from being chased by unwanted truths.

I used to think growth was elegant,
like a silver satin dress.
But, sometimes that dress needs
to be
torn,
   ripped,
      burned,
         destroyed.
Just to then be recreated into a cape.

Silence

Rickety palms cup glossy defunct eyes,
her sight an offering for Death,
who merely stares into her black longing sockets
in silence.

Blind, with only darkness now to lead,
she panics and begins to sever joints and cartilage.
"Take any limb you desire," she begs in toil.
"Just allow me to depart from this mortal coil."
but Death merely stares at her self-mutilated body
in silence.

A desperate last attempt, she picks at her stitches,
letting bloody seams fall, her flesh now exposed.
A dulled heart engulfed in her scorned fingers.
She collapses,
in silence.

And Death whispers
"You came asking for sympathy,
but I do not know that word.
You came asking for happiness,
but I do not know that word.

You came asking for death
but Death knows that's not what you wished.
It was rather a cease.
Of heavy eyes.
Of numbness.
Of flashbacks.
Of questioning.
Of not knowing how to go on.

And now you cannot go on."

And he turns his back
as a silent tear falls.

I am so thankful
that Death ignored my
pleas during my period of
darkness and delusion.

Not only am I alive.
But I'm happy.
And I'm happy to be alive.

Turns out pain is not as permanent
as it wants you to believe it is.

The Word

Transient

must never get lonely.

It is never far from home.

Symphony

I may be composed of broken trumpets blaring
and violins stuck on the flattened fifth,
but all symphonies begin in chaos.

Grown From Dirt

My fingers have been sterile lately,
lacking the grime
from a malfunctioning mind.

Now don't get me wrong—
I don't miss this mental soot
that's covered me for so long.
I have cleaned
every crevice with language,
prescriptions and tunnel vision.

I imagine a blooming flower
is also afraid to leave the dirt.

Your Ravaged Painting

The venue emptied as we spoke.
My hair white, your hair black,
like a chess board, pawns lined up neatly,
ready for battle.

I leaned against the wall,
imagining it crumbling under my shoulders,
drywall sinking into a giant black hole,
sucking me in and stretching my limbs
until I was nothing but a piece of white thread.
The things anxiety makes you imagine.

And we exchanged colorless words
as the occasional somebody would
ask you to sign their album, or take a photo.
A flash, a veiled smile, a raging black hole.

I think you felt it, too: the want
for more but not knowing
which pieces to move.
So you unexpectedly told
me how you found her alone
like a painting, ravaged
with too much crimson and Valium.
I found the darkness sarcastic then.
Everything was still.

Scissors

Impulse thaws the gap
between steel and frozen skin.
A cut into reality, displacement of pain—
however you want
to sugarcoat it.

Leaky Faucet

Who is vacating my eyes,
leaving the faucet on and bleaching
all the trees?
I would splash into hundreds of pieces,
disappear like this, too, if I could.

My Straight Jacket

"I promise" you said,
with your usual five-star performance.
I always told you that you should be an actor.
You always told me I'd make a great writer,
the way I drew meaning out of the meaningless.

I probably looked awful then,
my voice weak and my eye bags stuffed.
Every night I would drive up and down 3 am streets,
blasting Metallica as cold sweat burned my irises.
I refused to blink, I was afraid that
once I closed my eyes,
you'd be there.
I was afraid that if I turned the music down,
I'd hear you, laughing.
So I kept driving, until the sun came to relieve me.

I think I tasted insanity for the first time then.
It reminded me of honey, the way it melted
over your tongue, seducing you into another spoonful.
Except it wasn't as sweet, and instead of
dissolving across my tongue
it dissolved my tongue.

But I had a moment of clarity that day,
when I finally asked if it was you,
sending me threats laced with honey.
Those perverted, disturbing, twisted threats.

"Of course not, I promise."
And I believed you,
as I slipped back into my straight jacket.

The Rotten Peach

I must have amber oozing from my armpits,
nectar eluding from my nail beds,
with all this saliva pooling at my feet.

But that's always how it goes:
they never stop to peel back the skin.
They just want to see and drool, get a taste,
like fruit flies to a rotten peach.

Vulnerability #2

I added sugar

to the sour potion.

Now, finally, see me.

Black Magic

Death is quite the magician.
His first act is one of disappearance, the victim,
wrapped in his bloody cape, poofed into the abyss.
Yet, the real black magic occurs at his second act,
when tears are conjured from the eyes
that refused to open until the coffin was filled.

Swimming/Drowning

I used to describe depression as drowning.
But, I think that's just what I wished it was.

Depression is actually swimming,
but the water is dark and thick, like hot blood.
At first it's frightening, you no longer
can move your arms as briskly and your legs
have become heavy with the extra weight.
So you kick and paddle and kick and paddle
denying that you could have ended up here.

But eventually your arms get tired.
So do your legs.
The attempts to pull yourself out
become less frequent,
it's exhausting fighting darkness.
The distorted pool isn't as scary and the chill
of the water isn't noticeable anymore,
you're used to it.

So, you just give in. You stop moving,
letting the blood envelope you, keeping you still.
But, depression has a wicked sense of humor
because instead of drowning
you're barely treading water,
staying just enough afloat
to see everybody else
swimming laps.

It's Been A Year

And somewhere between

delusion

and

forgiveness

I've allowed

the shadows

to lull me

to sleep.

Bottle Bound

I yearn for our disorderly dance
of parted lips and glass. I'll ignite
my esophagus, anger my organs
because don't worry, darling,
even screaming, I am bound to you.

Cemetery Revelations

Amid cement and ivy
I sat and pondered death.
I'd gotten quite fond of the taste
of the topic, but, sitting
in front of wooden boxes
eternally suffocated under dirt,
hesitant footprints and
(never to be seen) mementos-

It tasted bitter.

World Shattering Hips

Lord Wotton taught me that "to define is to limit".
As he sunk into his favorite velvet sofa
with ribbons of smoke exhaling,
he told of times when he wandered
as a violin, in constant
search of his melody.

And now I sit saturating
in the scent of coffee and the sound
of French tongue.
Wotton's words try to break through
my oblivion, but it isn't his wisdom
that shatters me. It's her hips. And smile.

And I suddenly realize,
I've never known my melody after all.

Coffee Cake Lovers

I've been here before.
Coffee cake and fidgeting fingers.
The tables are porcelain and cold,
warmed by two cups of tea.

Watching, hopelessly watching,
I stare through closed eyes
although I can feel their burn
right in my own chest.
"Weather is quite nice," the girl says.
"The rain isn't as bad as it will be later in the week,"
I reply, lacing my fingers under the table.

I want to scream and tell
the could-have-been-lovers
to pick up a knife and peel off
their stubborn rind!
To plunge their hands
into their own skulls and scoop out
whatever is actually in there
because it sure as hell isn't
pleasantries and tight smiles
and a god damn weather report!

But I don't.
I never do.
It's just the memory
of the half-eaten coffee cake.

Little Pill

Little pill,
why do they bash you?
Have they tasted your tincture?
Have they tasted my woe?

Your creators may be convicts,
but does that make you one, too?
Maybe with the wrong accomplice.
But what about when I am dreaming
of scissors and train tracks?
When I really need you?

Little pill,
I am sorry for their aversion.
Maybe one day they will see
that with each person,
growth is not uniform
and never will be.

The Intimate Chihuahua

I think I've always been afraid of intimacy.
I remember when my 9th grade boyfriend
wrapped his arms around me,
I felt as if I had just committed sin.
I thought about sprinting home that very moment,
scrubbing my skin pink and praying for redemption.
It was just a hug.

Or when my friends would huddle close,
exchanging hard words and soft eyes,
pulling emotions and truths from their innards-
my skin would become rigid while I cracked every knuckle.
The only thing in my innards was a box, padlocked.
I didn't know where the key was.
I usually cried that night.

My therapist says it has something to do with childhood,
which pisses me off. I'm an adult now, not a child.
I should be able to hug and kiss and fuck
without feeling like a god damn Chihuahua
with her tail between her legs, quivering
under the far corner of the dining room table
just because my lover called me his baby.

I think I've always been afraid of intimacy.
Or rather, I just never understood it.
Usually that's the reason Chihuahuas yelp anyways,
they don't understand that the big scary human
is just trying to help. But, I guess it's safer under the table,
where you don't have to take any bets.

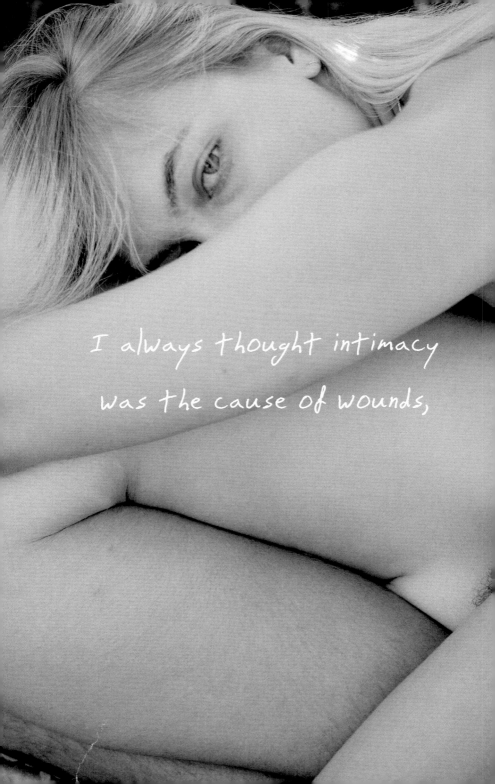

I always thought intimacy

was the cause of wounds,

but, I've finally learned
it's actually the salve.

Deeper Into The Labyrinth

Once again,
I became curious.

But in my defense,
how maddening it is
to ignore such
a persistent itch!
Truly, you must understand:
we all have this seek
sowed into our flesh.

Yes, I'm aware
my questioning drags
me, but once it begins,
how difficult to halt!

As if my innards
scream for answers,
refusing any
snakes,
apples,
monkeys
or even any
speck of stardust.

My innards demand certainty,
which is unattainable,
I know,
but sometimes
I become curious
and I try to defy-
dragging myself
deeper into the
labyrinth.

And Don't Forget To Be Yourself!

Raise your hand before you speak.
Say "Excuse me" if you burp.
Say "please" and "thank you".
Chew with your mouth closed.
Start an office job after school.
Don't talk about your breakup or
menstruation at your office job.
Don't talk about politics, ever.
Use a fork and knife, properly.
Don't dress promiscuously.
But don't dress too modest.
Drink cocktails, not beer.
Eat salads, not burgers.
Always be soft-spoken.
Don't lose it too young.
Don't lose it too old.
Wear bright colors.
Remain slender.
Be great in bed.
Don't be a slut.
Always smile.
Have long hair.
Have an ass.
Have boobs.
Look pretty.
Wear heels.
Cook well.
Love men.

Conform.

Zits

Leading with belligerent fingers,
you bend over the ivory sink, determined
to raid the red and pink reminders scattered
across the surface of your skin.
I lean against the door frame, eyes
trained on your reflection.
"Picking just makes it worse," I say.
"So?" Your cherry chin looks vexed.
"I like them.
They remind me
you're human."

Dear, Vicious Cycle

You are wine to me.
One sip and I endlessly
desire more.
Until I become sick.
and learn (temporarily).
and heal (temporarily).

A vicious cycle you are.
And a (drunken) one I am.

Time To Thaw

To admit one's mistakes
is not to burn,
but to thaw.

Malformed Fingers

It was 2:10 when she realized
what she did at 1:50 was wrong.
"If only my hands were the hands
of the selfish clock!" She thought.
She would have gladly bent
her fingers backwards, circling in tedium,
hoping to erase her wrongdoing.

So, she sat, rotting in regret,
planning her attack against the clock.
She fantasized of latching onto the metal rods,
dragging them against their glass tide,
waiting until 1:50 passed.
Only then would she be pleased,
even with her now malformed fingers.

When I first heard this tale,
I thought it was surely absurd.
Why kill time, trying to kill Time?
But now that I sit, with my own
guilt and conflicted conscience,
I contemplate bending my own fingers.

The Tell-Tale Half Smile

One day I'll find the courage
within myself (or a bottle of wine)
to ask if you think we're meant to be.

I know you well enough now
to know you'd give me one of those frowns
that isn't really a frown but rather
just another one of your cowardly masks.
We'd either be in the kitchen,
a pile of dishes between us- the perfect scapegoat.
Or maybe in the bedroom,
on opposite sides of the embarrassingly pristine bed.

And you know me well enough now
to know I'd give you that half smile
that isn't really a smile but rather
just another way of telling you
I already know the answer.

A Bite of Blues

My poetry is truly alive.
I am its every meal.
It digests what I cannot.

Immortal

To be immortal is not to remain breathing or being for eternity.
(Our fragile flesh could not maintain such a length, plus,
I would think enduring forever would become rather boring.)

I've seen the dead within strokes of paint and spirits in the cinema.
I've found immortality dancing in precisely paired words.
I've heard laughter in chapters and heartbeats in crescendos.

I don't know if I'll be fried to ashes or stuffed underground,
but I do know I will remain living through whatever
I create.

(Never stop creating.)

Acknowledgments

I know it sounds cheesy, but I have to say it- i'd be *nothing* without my followers, subscribers and supporters. I'm not sure if I'd even be publishing this book without all of you, so I have to give a massive, teary-eyed, uber-grateful thank you to every single one of you. I also would like to give a huge thank you to all the models that were kind and open-minded enough to let me photograph them, even though I am a very unexperienced, unorganized and sweaty photographer. And of course, all the people that reached out, willing to model for me or offer any form of help- you guys showed me such beauty in human nature, thank you. Another thank you to the several editors I worked with, my cover creator, May Phan, and the costumer service workers who always calmed me down when I would call at 12 am asking frantic questions about self-publishing. And thank you to everybody and anybody that gave me even the slightest bit of encouragement during the past 2 years of making this book. It was an emotional and turbulent ride and your words meant more than you will ever know.

Oh, and thank you to my cats for keeping me company while I wrote/ edited/paced throughout the night and for occasionally sitting directly on my keyboard when it was time for me to take a break/give pets.

I'm so thankful for all of you.

— C

cool humans in this book:

Models:

Alison Lee..........................ii
(@allisonleeee)
Alyssa Lumpee....................45
(@alyssalumpee)
Brianna McDonnell................20
(@_the_b_word_)
Chelsea Russell..................87
(@turkadurkk)
Emily Darling................vi, 75
(@groovyqurl)
Izzy Petyn.......................89
(@izzypetyn)
Karen Henriquez............i, 32, 33
(@vanessduh)
Khloe Quintana............7, 58, 59
(@khloequintana)
Minah Delane.....................17
(@xdarthlordx)
Nydeye Arame Fall................21
(@fallarame)
Sonia Leighton...................67
(@sonia.elsie)
Tatiana Salazar...............80, 81
(@tatiana.nickole)
Janai Burgess................50, 51
(@janai_marie)

Makeup Artist:

Alexis Gutierrez.............50, 51
(@allnaturalbarber)

Photographers:

Hanna Websterr.............vi, 74,75
(@tranquilseaaaas)
Camilla Petyn.........rest of photos

some important resources:

- **National Alliance on Mental Health Crisis Text Line:**
Text "NAMI" to 741-741

- **National Suicide 24/7 Prevention Hotline:**
Call 1-800-273-TALK (8255)

- **Self-Harm Prevention Hotline:**
Call 1-800-334-4357

- **Self-Harm Hotline:**
Call 1-800-DONT CUT (366-8288)

- **Hopeline Crisis Hotline:**
Call 1-800-442-4673

- **Teen Help Hotline:**
Call 1-877-332-7333
Or text "TEEN" to 839863

- **National Domestic Violence Hotline:**
Call 800-799-SAFE (7233)

- **National Rape and Sexual Assault Hotline:**
Call 800-656-HOPE (4673)

• **National Eating Disorder Alliance Helpline:**
Call 800-931-2237
Or text "NEDA" to 741741

• **Eating Disorder Helpline (mostly treatment referrals)**:
Call 1-866-418-1207

• **Trans Support Holine:**
Call 877-565-8860

• **"The Trevor Project" LGBTQ+ Support Hotline:**
Text "TREVOR" to 1-202-304-1200
Or call 866-488-7386

• **Substance Abuse and Mental Health Services Hotline:**
Call 1-800-662-HELP (4357)

• **National Addiction Hotline:**
Call 1-866-633-3239

#breakyoursilence

Made in the USA
Middletown, DE
26 October 2018